Bits and Peaces of Me:

Poetry From the Heart

By Jamie L. Eatmon Sr.

Bits and Peaces of Me:

Poetry From The Heart

© 2015 by Jamie L. Eatmon

First printing 2016

On The Rise Publishing has allowed this work to remain exactly as the author intended, verbatim, without editorial input.

ISBN-13: 978-1-945852-02-2
Library of Congress Catalog Number: Pending

PUBLISHED BY:
On The Rise Publishing
Georgia
Printed in the United States of America
Cover Design: Jamie Eatmon Sr.

Edited by: On The Rise Publishing Staff

Preface

Today I can honestly say, I am a blessed man. I have lived a blessed life. I have had losses in my life but what is most important today is that I have peace in my life. It is that peace that makes life worth living. It is that peace that enabled me to write this book *Bits and Peaces of Me: Poetry From The Heart.* The contents of this book were inspired by various episodes and stages of my life but it was the contentment at those points that allowed me to share the words that you are about to read.

The poems in this book were written over more than 40 years. They are each uniquely written yet they are strangely similar. The writings reflect a simplicity and innocence of a teenager and the complexity and drive of a man, "On The Rise." There is much to be read, pictured, entertained and understood. I must admit, I am a bit bias.

Therefore, you are encouraged to read and evaluate this book *Bits and Peaces of Me*, for yourself. This book is about love and strength. Growing up I was in love with love! Even now, despite the fact that I have failed at more relationships than I care to admit, I am still in love with love. There is no specific time or place that I can say I fell in love with love but I can say that I have always believed in the power of love.

Bits and Peaces of Me was inspired by the seasons of my life. Indeed there is a season for everything under the sun and here within this book, are poems inspired by the good, bad or indifferent seasons of my life.

I have both had and caused my share of disappointments. I have laughed in love, cried because of' love, sacrificed for love and most importantly learned to respect the power of love. As a teenager I began writing out of my innocence and later my ignorance. As my longing for love grew, so did my love for writing. The poems in this book are reflective of both that love and growth.

I was blessed by those who shared in my journey. Within this book, I reflect upon their specific moments in my life. I encourage them as well as you to read this book in its entirety.

If there is one lesson I have learned from love; one that I would hope you will get from this book, is that love is more powerful than any of the emotions; love is self-rejuvenating.

Dedicated

In Loving Memory of

My Madea, Amelia Brown-Hardy

My Mother, Georgia Mae Hardy-Eatmon

Dedicated to:

My children Tremaine, Jamie T., Tamarcus, Jamal, Jamika,

Lakenna, Jamie Jr., JaWanda and Mariah, my

Grandchildren and my loving wife Lady Antoinette.

About The Author

Jamie's journey as recorded in this book, is shared with the intention that you will be enlightened, inspired, encouraged and motivated but above all else, you will be empowered. Jamie Lee Eatmon Sr. in his own words is, "On The Rise". He feels that every aspect of his life has shaped and prepared him to be the man he is today. He was born in 1962, in the city of Eutaw, state of Alabama.

While being raised in the rural south, he was exposed to many of the southern woes but remained unscarred by them. He picked cotton alongside his grandmother, picked peas during his summers, drew water from a well, washed in a foot tub, slopped hogs and is quite familiar with the outhouse.

He was a member of the last class of the segregated Druid High School ('79) and a member of the first class of the desegregated Central High School ('80) in Tuscaloosa, Alabama.

Jamie's desire for writing was sparked at an early age. His first published work was printed in the 1979 issue of

Druid High School's newspaper, *Dragon Tales*. He was inspired by nursery rhymes he found in the pages of the family's encyclopedia set. It was in that same book that he recorded many of his first works around age eight. As he continued to write, writing became his passion, much of which you will find within the pages of this book, *Bits and Peaces of Me*.

He shares deep, revealing and intimate thoughts, views, values and desires. His writings are not merely creative words of poetry but a soulful outpouring of his heart.

Jamie discovered his Peace during the compilation of this book, a discovery that both challenged and motivated him to rise above the circumstances of life. His prayer is that his Bits and Peaces will help you to rediscover bits and peaces of your own life.

Today Jamie is a minister, husband, brother, father, grand-father and friend. He admits, "I have grown both callus and wiser however Bits and Peaces of Me, serves as a reminder to me, we must forever hold onto the peace of our being."

Acknowledgments

I would like to acknowledge everyone that has had an impact on and in my life. Many of the individuals whose contributions were most significant in my life are now my angels in Heaven.

I thank the individuals who remain, many may not even be aware of their contribution. Thanks Bertha, Barbara, Dorothy, Vel and Mom for your encouragement and contributions. Special thanks to Picola Smith whose talents are without bounds, Veronica Walker and Barbara Floyd who added the finishing touch to this work.

It is not the size of the contribution that most impacted my life but the character of the person. I thank you all, those from my past, those in my present and those in my future.

I would like to also thank and acknowledge you, the reader for sharing in the *Bits and Peaces of Me*.

Table of Contents

Gifts

The Bible informs us of the spiritual gifts that were given for our growth. Those gifts are made manifest and do operate in our person or being.

Ephesian 4:11-13 (KJV)

11 And he gave some ...
12 For the perfecting of the saints, for the work of the ministry, for the edifying of the body of Christ:
13 Till we all come in the unity of the faith, and of the knowledge of the Son of God, unto a perfect man, unto the measure of the stature of the fullness of Christ:

We should be grateful for the people in our lives, regardless of our thoughts or feelings towards, or for them. When we look over our lives we should be grateful for the storms, the sunshine and the rain keeping in mind that all things work together for the good of those who love the LORD, to them who are called according to His purpose.

Life's Journey

God gave us all two unavoidable paths to take,
A birth canal and a journey back to our Maker.

Between the two,
We are blessed with a lifetime to spend
Being a blessing to others,
Before meeting our Maker again.

There is a time to live and there is a time to die,
There is a time to laugh and a time to cry.
Life and laughter, death and tears,
May God sweeten our sorrows and comfort our fears.

God blessed us all
With something precious of His,
And we are eternally grateful
For the soul that has returned to Him.

Mama's Baby

I was born innocently into this life,

I had no idea where I was coming or why.

I remember how Mama pushed,

She pushed so hard that our insides gushed.

Yes, our insides for Mama and I were one.

But her pushing told me a change was about to come.

I was shoved down that long dark canal.

There was a light and with mama's help, I made it there.

I pushed with my head down between mama's legs.

It wasn't long before I reached a point of no return.

Mama must have known that I needed her help,

Cause she kept pushing and pushing I heard her yell.

With a shout, a moan, and a groan,

I found myself outside of my warm hollow home.

Someone grabbed my head, then my shoulders and my feet.

And before I knew it, a stranger was holding me.

I cried at the top of my voice.

I need my mother's touch, give me to her!

Mother of the Day
Dedicated In Memory of Georgia Mae Eatmon
My "Most Inspiring Mother".

I can't really call you an angel
> Though I hope you enter the pearly gates.

I can't really say you're heavenly
> Because you're down to earth in a lot of ways.

I won't say that you're sweet
> But that you're sweet in your own way.

Knowing you the way I do, I can say
> "The mere thought of you sweetens my day."

You're so very special
> In ways that you alone can be.

You've put so much
> Of yourself into the making of me.

I owe you so much more
> Than mere words can ever repay.

I give you this token
> Of my love to keep with you always.

I believe that Mother's Day was set aside
> For a mother to be honored by her child.

It would take a lifetime to give you due praise
> But for now "I wish you a Happy Mother's Day!"

Amidst the Storm

There is a sound heard in the utter silence of life.
There is a light that shines in complete darkness.
There is a place that only lonely lovers know
A place in life where longing hearts go to reminisce.
There is a possession that one never turns loose.
There is amidst all the lies in our life, a great truth.

There is treasure far more valuable than silver and gold,
There is a warmth that reaches you in the freezing cold.
There is a song that only the broken hearted knows,
There is a high place that only loving hearts can go.
There is a time and space void of here and now.

There is no such thing as an everlasting honeymoon,
There is only a growing love that must have room.
        Room to grow in Love, nurturing and strength,
        Room to breathe, shed leaves, weather storms,
        Room to wither, to die, to bud and to revive.

I have heard the silence;
        I have seen the light of darkness;
I know where the Hearts
        Of the Lonely retreat to reminisce.
I have heard the lonesome music
        And I have dance to its tune;
I know where there is
        No morning, night, evening or noon.

I've known love and I know
      The true essence of a honeymoon,
It's not about how we spend our time,
      It's all about giving room.
Giving room to the sun,
      That it might shine,
Giving room to the thunder,
      Yes it thunders sometimes.
Giving room to the season,
      For with seasons come change,
Giving room to our difference
      And yet loving each other the same.
Giving room to Peace,
      For it is a simple but precious thing,
Giving room to joy
      The Joy that the peace will bring.
Giving room to love,
      Time and time again,
Realizing that the only thing constant in life, is change.

**Honeymooning is
Surviving life's storm, again and again.**

A Picture

A picture is an eternally captured pose,
    The stillness of life
        Yet as live as a rose.
A picture is a memory that's timelessly framed,
    A captured moment,
        That goes forever unchanged.
A picture is a yesterday, kept for days to come,
    The moments shared with our
        Dear and precious loved ones.
A picture remembers what we hope to never forget,
    It is a present look at the past;
        A moment in time forever set.
A picture is a glance of those special times or someones,
    It's a look at places you've been
        or things you've done.
A picture is meant to be cherished for years to come,
    Turning easily forgotten moments
        Into most memorable ones.

Present Blessings

Presently we are far more blessed and are a far greater blessing to those around us than we realize. Because of fears of the future and what tomorrow may hold or bring we often take today for granted. This today is the day that the LORD has made. Rejoice and be glad in it.

1 Timothy 6:6-8 (KJV)

6 But godliness with contentment is great gain.
7 For we brought nothing into this world, and it is certain we can carry nothing out.
8 And having food and raiment let us be therewith content.

The words "Present Blessings", can best be appreciated and understood by contrast. For example, the contrast or opposite, would be past blessings, alluding to that which we had and lost along the way in life. When we realize that all things work together for our good, we then realize there really are no losses; only present or not present.

You're A Blessing

Oh how great is the day you were born,
What a blessed day it was,
For on that very day,
God manifested you unto the world.

Not because you were a gift
That your parents deserved
But because of your,
Unique ability to express His love.

My prayers are with you,
From the very depths of my heart,
I pray Peace and Blessings
Be upon you, Woman of God.

Your love has healing powers,
Something this world needs,
I thank the Lord for you,
Just knowing you has been a blessing to me.

Every Essence of You

If I only had a part of your love,
Enough it would never be.
If I had only a part of you,
You could never satisfy me.

If I could not see you,
Soul,
Mind,
Body
And Heart,
Then I would rather be blind and not see you at all.

If I could not feel all
Every essence of you.
My life would be incomplete
And our love untrue.

Here and Now

Do not forget the days,

The places and the times

That we have left behind.

Remember the moments

The time, the Space,

The Days of Our Lives

The Hidden Treasures

The real value of Here and Now

Love

There is love as you understand it and there is love as it is or ought to be. We tend to love from our heart and not from our spirit. In essence, most of what we practice or call love is based on our carnality. When we realize the power of love, we realize it is nothing short of spiritual and that most of us have yet to experience or know the power of love.

John 15:17-19 (KJV)

17 These things I command you, that ye love one another. 18 If the world hate you, ye know that it hated me before it hated you. 19 If ye were of the world, the world would love his own: but because ye are not of the world, but I have chosen you out of the world, therefore the world hateth you.

Love has the power to transform our very beings into something more beautiful and valuable than we can ever carnally see or imagine. We are to love everyone however, the relationship we have with others determines the degree and aspects of love we share with them. Man and woman in their relationship should love and prefer their oneself. Whereas we must all love and respect others as we do ourselves.

Remembrance of Your Comfort

Your eyes are like mirrors reflecting life to me,
In them I can see togetherness and reality.
Your embrace as secure as that of a mother's arms,
Surrounded by the presence of your unforgettable charm.
Your heart is like a clock to me,
Our hour grows nearer with its every beat.
Your tears are like precious blood flowing,
Not telling of your love but showing.
Your laughter is the happiest moment of the happiest day,
Not only sounding so beautiful but there's so much it says.

For instance,
"Yes I love you, I thought you knew,
Yes, I know, you love me too".

Boochie you can fuss, you can even get mad,
And leave if you want,
But I'm gonna be here when you get back... HUH!

Admiration

The heart cries out in ways
That only a heart can see.
It looks within a man,
Where pride would hide his plea.
I have seen you cry out,
I watched from a distant view,
Though I hush my heart,
In silence it cries out for you.
You may not have heard my crying
But surely you can see,
Though a world of others surrounds me,
I'm still lonely.
I do admire you… but more so,
I want you to understand,
Your Friend, I am
But the eyes that see you
Are those of a man.

Heart Sent

I took up my pen
In an attempt to express myself,
I'm trying to say,
"I love you," if nothing else.

I want to say,
"Nowadays, things aren't the same,"
My arms cry out to hold you,
As my lips whisper your name.

"I love you; I love you;
I love you my dear,"
If my heart could speak,
Those are the words you'd hear.

Since my heart has no voice
Or pen of its very own,
This is from my heart,
"I shall love you a lifetime long."

Life's Treasure

What shall I say of this wonderful thing,
Except that it's so out of reach yet so easily seen.
It's so hard to come by
And yet even harder to understand.
Though it's limited in quantity, it's always in demand.
This wonderful, wonderful thing
That we all are in need of,
It's so hard to explain,
So let's just call it Love;
It's more than the touch,
Of tender hands, this tender thing.
It's as small as a smile
And the warmth it amazingly brings.
This wonderful thing
Has been defined in so many ways,
It's the most valuable treasure
I have found in all my days.
This here Love,
This here wonderful blessing known as Love,
It's found in many hearts,
Yet you can only give it from yours.
What have I said of this wonderful thing called Love?
Love is a rarity not often found but often spoken of
Like the crying voices of poets.
Hear me as I moan
If you have found Love
Then treasure it for a lifetime long.

Love Always

"Somebody said it many, many years ago, that when love
gets in your blood, you find it hard to let go." Natalie Cole

The beauty of a flower,
       Says nothing for the fragrance thereof,
Likewise, saying "I Love You"
       Could never express my love.

               I give you my time,
              I give you my treasure,
            But beyond any measure,
              I give you my love.

I give you my love,
       You know not the fullness thereof.
I can begin to tell you,
       I can even try to express,

            But when it comes to speaking of love,
             Love speaks for itself.

I say to you "I Love You,"
       As sweet as those words seem,
They are far from
       Exactly what it is I mean.

The day will come
       When I must go or I will have gone,

Be it due to death or distance,
Remember, my love lives on.

Words may cease,
The flowers may die.
Memories may fade
And the sun may not shine.
But rest assured;
You can count on this love of mine.

Who is to say
If this love is right or wrong?

Should I leave you or should you leave me?
This you should know.
Whether or not this love was meant to be,
Matters not to me,

In my heart I shall love you forever more.

Acquainted

There's so many things about you,

    That I may never come to know.

Then there's the little simple things,

    That can't help but stand out so.

Your smile, as warm and beautiful as can be.

Your laughter is evidence of your warm personality.

To look at you is to see,

A woman hard on the outside,

With feelings that run ever so deep.

I'll never know you

    The way I would like to

But with each passing moment,

    I feel a little closer to you.

Love Undefined

Love is so funny you know,
It's as hard to hold on to
As it is to let go.
I find it hard to understand,
How such a cherish-able thing can hurt so.
Love is the laughter,
Love is the tears,
Love is everything we've experienced, over the years.
Love is the hurt,
Love is the pain,
Love is said to be a many of splendid things.
Love is oftentimes better if left undefined,
For I believe it to be a matter of the heart,
And not of the mind.

Love

Settle not for beauty

   It is said to be skin deep.

Settle not for ugliness

   It is said to go straight to the bone.

Settle not for a love of depth or width

   But rather for a love,

That will last a lifetime long.

Sea of Love

My heart shall always love you,

As my arms long to hold you.

My soul shall cry out for you,

If ever I find I am without you.

My feelings for you are as strong and as deep,

As a river flowing into a Sea of Love.

Pooling into the deepest and innermost memories,

See how still, runs these waters of Love.

The voice of my soul is like the sea gull,

Forever crying out in search of your love.

Echoing waves in search of your distant shore,

To flood your heart, with my unending love.

"I LOVE YOU; I LOVE YOU"

From the ship to the shore.

My Flower

"Roses are Red," So the saying says,

But my flowers

Are memories of yesterday.

Of a love like a flower in full bloom,

So beautiful, with its winter approaching soon.

Once winter set in,

My flowers lost their leaves.

My flowers, though now barren,

Are still flowers indeed.

Looking back on yesterday,

I see a flower that was,

Today I envision tomorrow's flower

As one blooming in Love.

Your Flower

In a World of "I Understand..."
There are few that really do.
Though they can see your struggle,
They'll never know what you go through.

Every day of life we are given 24 hours,
To accomplish what we will or may,
We make our way through time's corridor
And we are blessed with another day

There's a secret the tombstone conceals,
It reveals everything, except for how one lived.
Life is a canopy of interwoven moments of time,
Patterned into memories, embroidered on our mind.

No doubt you shall be remembered,
The question is, "By whom and for what?"
The answer is a simple one,
"By those who were touched by your love".

Someone, once said, "Give me my flower",
He requested, "Give it, while I yet live".
I wish you a long and prosperous future,
Please accept this,
"Your Flower", while you yet live.

My Sweetheart

If I don't receive a thing on Valentine's Day,

I won't be disappointed, you must understand.

Because the one gift given from your heart,

Satisfies my every desire and all my demands.

I thought I would take time out to say,

Just how happy I'll be on Valentine's Day.

To be with you is truly gift enough for me,

It will be the best Valentine's Day I could hope to see.

Candy is sweet and I do enjoy its taste,

But sweets alone can't bring a smile to my face.

Really, truly, sincerely, I'm trying to say,

Your Love alone, is gift enough for me any day.

Treasurable Memories

Who can capture a rainbow,
The beauty of its sight?
Who can capture the warmth of the day,
Or calm of night?

How long does a flower,
Bloom Before it withers out of season?
These are uncapturable,
As do flowers die without reason.

Some things can't be handled or held;
The things eyes rarely see.
For instance, the warmth I feel
Every time you are near to me.

The tenderness of your touch,
I see and I feel,
Yet my eyes and hands,
Have never sensed such.

I speak of a few precious moments
Which I've come to treasure so,
I've never captured a rainbow
Nor found its pot of gold.

37

I've never captured the warmth of day,
Nor the calm of night,
I've seen flowers bloom and die,
And come Spring bud into life.

These are not thoughts of that,
Which are to be handled or held,
They are expressions of the past
With enough life to be relived.

I'm trying to relate to you
What your memories are to me
And how with each new day
I renew them daily.

Though life so quickly passes me by,
As you have come and gone,
The very remembrance of you,
"I will treasure a lifetime long."

Urgent Message

It's very important,
That I get this message across to you.
It's quite urgent,
That this message somehow gets through.
There is this special something,
That I've been wanting to say,
It concerns you in my life,
And how I'm hoping you'll stay.
I've said it in poetry,
But you found only rhyme in my poems.
I was hoping you would have felt it,
In the comfort of my arms.
I've sent you letters
But there's only so much words can say
But I keep trying,
Hoping that you'll get my message someday.
When this day is gone
And my tomorrows have all passed away,
My last wish will be,
That you realize what I have tried to say.
I leave this urgent message
Just in case you fail to realize,
"Sharing your love, is the most pleasant part of my life."

Inspired by Love

Love is far more powerful than we realize. Love is light and it is the only thing capable of eliminating or transforming life's darkness or hate. Today we live in a society where our hearts are all too often given along with our bodies, in the name of Love.

Unfortunately, it is that mindset and that love that causes unrepairable damage in the lives of all too many. Today we are challenged to let Love's light shine and to transform ill emotions into true love.

John 5:1-3 (KJV)

Whosoever believeth that Jesus is the Christ is born of God: and everyone that loveth him that begat loveth him also that is begotten of him.
By this we know that we love the children of God, when we love God, and keep his commandments.
For this is the love of God, that we keep his commandments: and his commandments are not grievous.

When we discover or rediscover the love that we should have in our heart towards the Lord, we are better able to understand the love we should have towards our neighbor. Love is the key to a brighter future let your love light shine.

Your Love

Your love has become more than a necessity,
It alone satisfies my ever-increasing need.
A need that I ignored up until I met you,
Since meeting you, my dreams are coming true.

Your love is a sight
Pleasing throughout my soul,
Your love is a beauty,
That eyes alone cannot behold.

Your love is a treasure;
I'll value my whole life through,
I've never found a love,
So precious as I've found in you.

If I could have only one pleasure throughout life,
It would be you loving me
As my God-given wife.
If tomorrow comes
And you and I are not together,
I'll spend my life longing for your love;
I will love you forever.

Love Song

For of all the languages known,

       Love is hardest to understand,

The precious communication,

       Between a woman and a man.

It's like music in the heart,

       A soul stirring Love song,

Let it fill your heart,

       With its melody and sing along.

Let It Be

If there is one thing
I never want to lose,
That one thing without a doubt
Is definitely you.
I realize my loving you,
Doesn't make you love me?
But I know that you do,
For how else could it be?
That you my love,
Have come this far with me,
Our love will continue to grow,
"Just Let It Be."
I realize longing for you
Doesn't make you long for me,
But I know that you do,
For how else could it be?
That through clouds of darkness,
I can still see
A picture-perfect love,
If we will just "LET IT BE"!

Giving My Love To You

Like waters in a stream,
My Love flows without measure.
To bathe you in my love,
Is my life's long pleasure.
You are comparable with
The warmth of a summer day,
A day so lovely that I shall remember you always.
The beauty of a flower,
Can be seen by those near and afar.
You my love, are the one flower,
That I cherish within my heart.
The rose is surrounded by the protection of thorns
But you my flower, need no protection from these arms.
Words alone have failed,
To get my message across to you.
Though it is seemingly impossible,
This is an all-out effort to,
Say I love you and how much I do care.
Let me assure you,
Should our love enter a state of despair,
Should division come tomorrow
And I find myself alone.
I will find comfort in "remembering,"
If I can't hold you in my arms.

Let Me Show You

It's not so important
How long I've known you,
As it is how well
I have come to know you.
Measure not my love
So much on how often I tell you,
Rather measure my love
By how much I show you.

Elements of Love

Silence your thoughts,

Still your emotions,

Feel the flow of my love,

Battling like waves in the ocean.

Rushing to and fro,

From oceans depth to yonder shore,

Battered and driven are my emotions.

Calm, deep and yet raging like the ocean.

Our love lies stranded

Somewhere on a distant shore.

My longing rides the waves,

In search of our love, both near and far.

My thoughts are in the breeze,

That blows gently against your face.

My desires are in the sun,

That warmly caresses you each day.

My passion grows for you,

Spilling over like the morning dew.

I am the thunder and lightning;

I am the heat and the cold.

I am full of unharnessed power,

That flows within my soul.

I Am the night

Though I say not a word.

I Am the day

Proclaimed by the birds.

I Am That I Am,

Not knowing what I am to be.

I am the larva,

The cocoon and the butterfly,

Desperately in search of my destiny.

I am older than time itself,

I helped create the world,

Now I must raise myself.

If you can understand

What it means to search for self,

Then I ask this of you,

Be a burden if you must

But realize, you must also be a help.

Someone I Know

I have a friend one I'll never forget
And according to her "You don't know me yet".
She's not far from wrong
And even closer to being right.
One can only see the stars,
If he gazes into the night.
The light of the day is provided by the sun
And night must fall, before the morning comes.
Is not the night but half a day without light,
For what is day without the presence of night.
I am but a whisper in the darkness,
Looking for the light.
The day that I can say
I have withstood the night
You say, "You don't know me", Oh, but I do.
This is the dawn of our relationship;
I'm awaiting a brighter you.

Small Talk

What started as routine conversation,
Left me longing to listen forever more.
I met the beautiful you on the outside
But it was the inner you, I've come to adore.

      I listened closely to your depths as you spoke,
      I became intoxicated as I savored your words.
      I found myself looking into your eyes,
      There I found the spirit of the un-caged bird.

I know that you know why the caged bird sings,

I felt it in your words, as though your lips were wings.

Each one resounding, "Life has made her a Queen!"
I bowed as I listened, subjected to your inner being.

      On the outside we appear as that we wish to be,
      But if we are to get acquainted, we must dig-deep.

      Dig beyond the outer surfaces, we all tend to grow,
      Dig until we find the Who, that dwells at our core.

I don't mean to sound like the outer you is a waste,

But I want to get close enough to share your inner space.

You are a flower, be it blossoming, or as a bud,

I want to know the You, that is, shall be and was.

      Life is a fortress if you will, a forest of trees,
      In life we behold the presence of what use to be.
      The past is in the past, but it helps us understand,
      Why 2-minute conversations never come to an end.

Come With Me My Angel

Come with me my Angel, Come travel with me,
Travel with me as I explore our present reality.
Come! Close your eyes and open your mind,
There is a Truth that we must somehow find.
Come now if you will, step outside of yourself,
Come into my world so you can see a little better.
I am on a journey to a destination that only God knows,
Look now and behold there are many paths in the road.
Behold my heart, It is the most valuable thing I own,
Notice how it and my Soul comes together as one.
I know this is nothing new; you just never saw it before.
Come now that we are here, let's look a little farther.
Come! here is where I reason and feel.
Watch your step, Strange as it may seems,
I still have unexplored depths.
Look there, rainbows of emotions,
Amidst clouds of confusion.
And that body of water,
Those are tears I've cried in seclusion.
You may not know it but all that you now behold,
Makes me the man you've come to know.
Come there's a deeper side of me,
My deeper and innermost space.
See I am indeed a Temple of God
And we are entering my most Holy Place.
Here is where God and I meet,
Where I have suffered great victories,
And even more important, many defeats.

I am man; I am flesh; I yearn and I lust;
But I am Spirit and in God I Trust.
I do battle here, my weapons are not carnal,
The Word serve as my army and my Armor.
This is both my birthplace and my grave,
Here I am both my Master and my Slave.
It is from here that I make my outcry,
It is here where I choose to live or die.
I invited you here in hope you would see,
That every day is indeed a battle for me.
See I live within and you look from without,
I engage in struggle, when you question and doubt.
Come now, my emotion are stirring underneath,
Let's move on, before thoughts rise from the deep.
This concludes our journey; I hope you now understand;
You may see me struggling,
But my battles are won within.
Many do question my thoughts
And the expressions on my face,
But unlike you they have never
Visited my Most Holy Place.
Many shall read and shall not understand,
For it takes an intimacy to know the inner man.
So, my Angel, you now know me,
Without and within,
And I pray God reveals to you,
"I am indeed your friend."

I Miss You

Just how much do I miss you?
In your heart you must surely know.
For my heart cries out to you,
"Oh my Love, how I miss you so."
As I sit perched on sorrow's step,
I'm deeply troubled in heart and mind.
As I search within myself for words to say,
Just how I feel at this moment in time.
I search for words in the silence of thought,
Yet only memories come rushing back, one by one.
I search the very inner chamber of my heart,
For some verbal expression to express my love.
I love you; no corridor in time can change that,
My love shall accompany you, no matter where you are at.
There are so many things I wish we could say and do,
I guess I'm really trying to say, "I miss You".

My Sunshine

In the darkness of lonesome moments,
That somehow cloud the light of my mind.
I find myself momentarily lost,
Caught between the moments of time.
My mind holds the key,
To all that I Am and Who I Am to be
And in those moments of darkness
I often find myself losing sight of me.
No man is an island unto himself,
Life has proven those words true.
For every mountain or valley in my life,
There was someone that helped me through.
When we experience eclipses, in our life,
Those someone's come shining through.
You are one of those someone's,
You would be surprise who looks to you.
You are the light of peace to some,
A ray of hope to others.
In the dark and lonesome moments,
The sunlight burns its way through.
In life we will experience an eclipse or two,
The key is having the strength to endure.
Memories of you illuminate my mind
There is peace in your presence, "My Sunshine."

BLUE

I love the color Blue,

It describes my relationship with you.

Let me relate the word Blue to you.

B is for your Beauty,

    Something you very much bare.

L is for your Loyalty

    And your loving care.

U is for the Understanding,

    That got us through the despair,

E is for Ever,

    The Everlasting Love we share.

Growing Interest

I met a woman, at an interesting point in time.
Even more interesting, is how she lingers in my mind.
The time was mutual and common was the meeting place,
I have yet to determine how she ended up in my space
There was no door to knock on and no doorknob to turn,
No sidewalk or beaten path to follow or walk upon.
I had forgotten the place,
As though it was something long gone,
But there she stood; I'm still wondering
Where did she come from?
I opened to door to make sure she wasn't lost.
She presented her token, Friendship at all cost.
Oh, how it glittered, Friendship,
A Jewel ever so rare,
I welcomed her in,
And the interest grew from there.

Wisdom

Wisdom, as though it was treasure is valued among men. According to the world, men who appear foolish, are said to lack wisdom. According to the Bible, men of the world, who are thought to be wise, are foolish before the LORD. Wisdom as significant as it is, is most valuable, when and where there is understanding.

Wisdom is the discerning gauge between serenity and courage. Without the proper application of wisdom, men who consider themselves wise, might very well come across as being foolish. We should always pray for wisdom in every aspect of our lives, particularly when it comes to matters of the heart.

1 Corinthians 3:18 (KJV)

18 Let no man deceive himself. If any man among you seemeth to be wise in this world, let him become a fool, that he may be wise.

Proverb 4:5-7 (KJV)

5 Get wisdom, get understanding: forget it not; neither decline from the words of my mouth.
6 Forsake her not, and she shall preserve thee: love her,

and she shall keep thee.

7 Wisdom is the principal thing; therefore, get wisdom: and with all thy getting get understanding.

When confronted with issues in life, we must use wisdom and ultimately accept matters or exercise the courage to change them. We can only do so through the proper application of wisdom and love.

Wisdom has taught me that **Love is the key to a brighter future**, I encourage you to wisely let your Love light shine.

Ancestral Knowledge (On The Rise)

You are not alone; you never have been.
It's just that you're always looking out and never within.
No, the world won't love you;
It never did, and never will.
See, the world has nothing to offer
But you have everything to give.
My child hope is a lantern,
Faith is a light,
You must hold on to both of them,
If you are to survive the night.
The world is a dark place, it gets cold sometimes
But look within,
For the warmth of the light of your mind.
Look to me,
For I am truly alive and well,
Just as you were before you were born to live.
I am your roots,
The Seeds from which springs Family trees,
I am in every Branch,
I'm in the bark and I am in every Leaf.
I was you, before you were
And now you are me.

I am your past,
Just as you are the present for me,
We have come here together
For those who are yet to be.
When my life seemed hopeless,
All I could do was look to you.
You were my lantern of hope;
You gave me strength to endure.
So now my child,
It is time we unite as one,
See the race before you
Is one that only you can run.
Be encouraged my child,
As you take the baton.
You must be swift and wise
And remember to always look inside.
For years, I have been silent,
But never again,
Now that we have found each other,
Let the race begin.
Take the baton knowing that I Am at your side
And that "nothing can hold you back,
When you are On The Rise."

Love Incomprehensible

Your heart could have no vision,

Your mind could have no thought.

My pen could never write it,

So many times the words I've sought.

I'm saying " I Love You"

Just as I've done before,

But words alone simply can't describe my Love.

There are those special things I may say and do,

Which are only a fraction of my Love for you.

Ignorance

Oh, how you have seasoned my life,
With your increasingly bitter taste.
Though you speak in many voices,
You can never hide your face.

I probably shouldn't address you,
In hope that you'd just go away
But you just can't help being yourself,
An undesirable voice with a familiar face.

I speak to others constructively
But you won't let them hear a word I say.
I try to be patient with others
But lose them at the sight of your face.

You dare to enter my home
And speak to me in disrespect.
It is your will that I should grow cold,
Filled with envy and regret.

You speak through the mouths of men,
Who consider their hearts nor souls.
Not knowing that although it's their mouth,
It's your face that shows.

When I hear your voice,
I can only listen to you and stare
Because if I spoke my mind,
I would probably find you there.

I wish I could label you,
In a way the whole world could see.
Then you would not be heard
And you would then cease to be.

Go on to the next little voice,
Engage his mouth, speak his mind
And once you have spoken,
Maybe he will know you the next time.

Somewhere down the line you'll find,
Men given to thinking before speaking.
Then I shall not see your face nor hear you speak.
But hear the words of the humble and the meek.

An should I open my mouth to offend,
May I hold my words and consider the matter again.

See You Tomorrow

When my tomorrow has come
And your today is at hand.
Yesterday will become,
Simply a moment in the past.
Yesterday will be but a memory,
A sentimental glance looking back.
With the coming of tomorrow,
Today shall come to an end at last.
Look upon today and adore her sight,
She's merely a yesterday, a fading light.
Upon tomorrow's coming,
Today is to be sacrificed,
Giving yesterday a new life.
Of tomorrow, I cannot foretell,
Except that though it isn't, it is.
I've searched for tomorrow in so many days,
Only to find yesterday amidst today.
Yesterday I looked upon today,
Thinking it was tomorrow that I saw.
As a result of my searching, I now believe,
Tomorrow is the day that I won't see at all.
When my tomorrow has come,
And your today is still at hand
And I am but a sentimental glance in the past,
Remember me,
For when your tomorrow has come,
Upon that day I will see you again.

Soul At Large

Take my hands,
They've done more right than wrong,
Take my feet,
They're weary, tired and worn.
Take my eyes,
They've seen many wonderful things.
Take my ears,
They've heard the melody the mockingbird sings.
Take my legs,
They're slim but yet stout.
Take my arms,
They've let many, in and out.
Take my head,
Only give it a place to rest.
Take my body,
It is a little worn,
But it's a body none the less.
Take my mind,
Dare not seek what I know.
Take my heart
And tell me why it beats so,
Take my every and all, all but my Soul,
For it is the one thing,
Which this world cannot hold.

Backache

I have so much upon my shoulders,
The load gets heavier by the day
But rather then buckle my knees,
I'll stand here 'til my backaches.
I've wiped tears from my eyes with one hand,
While I held my patience in the other.
I have cried out in a weary voice,
Which in the toils of the day were smothered.
Though my shoulders are not so broad,
They carry the load I must bear each day.
Though my knees have grown weak,
I shall not stumble along my way.
Daily the weights are added one by one,
The less I can take the more I get.
And as much as my backaches,
My back hasn't broken yet.

Distance

As I lay in bed listening to the radio,
I remember the sweet love songs,
Soft and slow.
As I awaken and behold another day,
My thoughts are of you,
Soo close, yet soo far away.
I close my eyes in rest and call it sleep,
Setting aside all
But the one treasure I hope to keep.
It's a collection of tender memories,
Sweet and warm,
That my heart embraces
And for which my arms yearn.
Though miles would try to create,
Distance between us two,
You are not so distant,
That I can't spend time with you.

Familiar Thoughts

Should this world grow cold,

 There are thoughts to warm my soul.

 Should my day grow empty and dark,

There are thoughts to lighten up my heart.

Should I be forsaken by those around me,

My thoughts will satisfy my social needs.

If I should lose everything that I own,

I shall be rich in life with my thoughts alone.

Gratifying are my thoughts of you,

Stored moments until I need them for use.

I keep those thoughts in my heart and mind,

That way you are with me at all times.

With each thought I realize I love you so

And each passing thought makes me love you more.

My thoughts have been such touching memories,

Filled with the familiar powers of Family.

Hard Luck

Hello my world, how are you doing?

Me, I'm just fine.

Tell me World, why are you so harsh all of the time?

All of your troubles and worries,

Why make them mine?

Why do you feel I must lose,

All of the time?

I try to do what's right

But I somehow go wrong.

Ending where I started,

Questioning, how far have I come?

World, you've really shown

Your rough side to me,

I can't help but wonder,

How the other side must be.

Sometimes I feel that,

There's a world of trouble on my back.

But as you know, I still press on,

You can't hold me back.

See World I'm not at all happy

or close to content,

As for hard luck,

One day you'll wonder just where he went.

I Looked Back

I stop and I look back,

Still I press onward;

Further and further I travel,

From where I wanna be.

I look back,

It's so comforting,

Still I press onward;

Ahead in front of me,

Not knowing what's to be.

So many encounters along the way,

Still I press onward,

Losing sight of tomorrow,

Clinging to yesterday.

I can't really go;

Still I press onward,

In the direction of uncertainty,

Looking back at where I wanna be.

I can only greet today

As I press onward to meet tomorrow.

Of yesterday I can only say,

Looking back,

I lost so much of me along the way.

Lord Help The Children

LORD help the children of the world today,

Help them LORD, for we all need help these days.

Especially the children, for whom I now pray,

Those Oh LORD who so easily lose their way.

LORD help the children,

LORD hear my humble plea,

Help them that are LORD

And them who are yet to be.

The troubles of this world,

No child needs to know,

Show them the way LORD,

And be with them as they go.

LORD bless their souls,

And dry their weeping eyes,

LORD comfort them that mourn,

Oh LORD hear their cries.

LORD help the children in this old world today,

Take their hand Oh LORD

And show them the way.

Help the children Oh LORD,

For whom I now plead,

I pray for the children,

For life is hard indeed.

LORD help us all,

For we all need help now and then,

And In Jesus name I pray,

"God Bless The Children."

Reach For The Sky

Someone once said to me,
"The Sky is the limit."
Little did they know;
They were limiting my reach.
I heard them
And I even believed them for a while.
Then one day I grew up,
I stopped thinking like a child.
Today the clouds are a bit higher
Because I lifted up the sky.
The sky has no limits
And I too, am limitless now.
I have no limits;
I know no bounds.
Yes, the sky was the limit
But I lifted up the sky.
Gravity holds me bound,
Yet my thoughts are my limits.
I was told to reach for the sky,
I did and I raised it even higher.

Remembrance

Hello my love, how have you been?

It's me, your old love and forever friend.

It seems so long ago, since I saw you last.

It is so strange how time comes and goes so fast.

I guess I'm addressing the fullness of remembrance,

As I look back at the memories one by one.

My, the women I've loved, how they've come and gone.

Leaving behind them memories to forever linger on.

Remembrance, my most dependable friend,

You've been so pleasant time and time again.

There are so many people you bring to mind,

Without you, I can't imagine how I'd spend my time.

Life Expectancy

Who's this waiting so impatiently

To see this side of life?

Is it a doctor, a lawyer

or simply a reader of poems?

So full of life,

The child will eagerly come into the world

And as he draws his first breath,

To life He will belong.

Into the world,

Another innocent life comes,

Entering into a race

That he alone can run.

As parents we give them birth

As The LORD gives them life

And I a prayer, that in the darkness

They will find the light.

The hurdles of life,

The troubles of the world,

Enemies known and unseen,

Are all a part of the race.

There will be dismay,

Weariness and moments of despair.

I know a way, not an easy way

And I pray He finds it.

A way that not everyone can travel,

For some do faint.

Mom and Dad tell him,

LORD bless him with understanding

To know that the race can be won

Though it is demanding.

Once he comes into the knowledge of life,

May he endure,

All that is set before him in the race,

Until his spirit returns home again

To its heavenly place.

Struggles

We struggle in life to reach our goals,
>We are full of desire, yet empty in our souls.
We search for happiness almost everywhere,
>Thinking we've found it, only to find it's not there.
Children all struggle as they attempt to be men,
>Wishing over and over they were a child again.
As children we struggle to become someone,
>Imitating others and the things they've done.

Fathers struggle both the old and the young,
>If you like the blues, just listen to their songs.
Fathers struggle, some to remember, some to forget,
>For some, Fatherhood is only something to regret.
Some mothers struggle providing for their sons,
>They are mother and father all wrapped in one.
Mothers struggle trying to replace dear old dad,
>Who took with him her dreams, all that she had.

Look at the children slowly growing up to be men,
Look at the mothers and how they're dreaming again.
Look at the fathers, mothers' children now fully grown,
It's time we the children gave love a happy home.

Ten and Seven

Now that I'm ten and seven and I know life's no joke,
Old man time takes a life with every second stroke.
Now I'm ten and seven that's young you know,
But now I can see things clearer than before.
I look at the prejudice, I see a little in you,
But don't worry, it happens to every three out of two.
Prejudice hurts; oh but you say not you,
It's something you've learned to live with, well I have to.
That same old prejudice that lived so long before,

He will probably live tomorrow and forever more.
Old man Prejudice sees your kids with the same old eyes,
He will have his hand in everything that he tries.
You know I'm ten and seven, and a black child at that,
This is not a white or black world, can't you see that.
I have not much knowledge but I do have a little to tell,
It's neither false nor true, my opinion is what it is.
Our history books go quite a ways back in time,
It speaks of an enslaved race, none other than mine.
History tells us that we were brought here in slave ships,
The golden valuable stone, of which I'm only a chip.
I have no remembrance of a homeland or crossing a sea,
But I know in my soul that I'm still not truly free.
We slaved in the fields while they were beating our backs,
You may have conducted the train; but we laid the track.

Expense Account

The rarest of treasures, is taken for granted each day.
We rarely consider the price of it, or just who must pay.
Many things in life have values, far less than their cost.
Others are simply taken for granted, until they are lost.
One who spends wisely will consider the added expense.
Because everything in life is taxed, speaking in a sense.
I purchased your friendship with sincerity and concern,
Sealed it in a trust, and wrapped it using care as yarn.
It wasn't expensive, considering the amount I had to pay
But I knew the friendship would be taxed someday.
Since its date of purchase, its value far exceeds its cost,
No matter how much it's taxed it will not suffer a lost.
Friendship is a joint account, we share in the expense.
It is constantly being taxed by others, speaking in a sense.
When I made my purchase, I had no Idea of the final cost,
I made my purchase, with no intentions of suffering a lost.
Friendship will be taxed, there is an expense, no doubt
But it's not so costly because friendship is a joint account.

It's All Music

Somebody play me a love song,
In the down-home bluesy way.
Somebody look in Mama's old records
And find a love song to play.
I want love to embrace me
And the blues to hold me tight.
I want to hear an all-mixed-up melody,
That sounds the way I feel tonight.
Play me the blues because my baby's gone,
I want to hear its sad and lonely tune.
Play me a love song, sweet, slow and long,
Let it play all night, until the morning comes.
My heart's in turmoil like never before,
It hurts to hold on, yet I can't let go.
She means so much to me, till it hurts my soul,
Wisdom says to let go, but desire says take hold.
I can feel the love simmering within me,
And yet the blues waxes my inside cold.
Everything within me wants to hold on to her,
Yet my heart cries lovingly, "Please let her go".
I sit here replaying the words of hope said to me,"
Some of the things we love most, we must set free
And it will return to us, if it was meant to be."

God's Angel

God has angels He dispatches them at will,

He sends them to comfort, Restore and Heal.

When you are troubled in heart

And your hope is growing dark.

When you've cried unto God in prayer

And you still can't find Peace anywhere.

Stand, just be faithful, continue to hold on and pray.

Trust and believe in your heart

And surely God will send an angel your way.

Don't miss your angel searching for wings,

Don't miss your angel searching your dreams.

For angels encompass us about each and every day,

Pray and be faithful, God sends an angel your way.

An angel without wings, outside your dreams,

God knows your needs, even before you plead.

Hold on, be ye steadfast and faithfully pray,

Trust in God, He will surely send an angel your way.

Trust God and be true, till your angel comes to you.

Never Regret Nor Forget

Never regret giving your love to me,

Never regret seeing with your heart,

What eyes couldn't see.

Never regret the pain and hurt,

You might have come to know.

Never regret those moments,

When you felt so low.

Never regret the tears,

That might have fallen from your eyes.

Never regret for once you do,

Your regret are no longer a part of you.

Don't forget the love you gave,

How it was returned.

Don't forget the trust,

That you so easily earned.

Don't forget the pain,

And that it was shared by two.

Don't forget the troubles,

That love brought you through.

Don't forget, there's no use trying,

For you bury the dead and not the dying.

Always remember how we shared things,

Things both great and small.

Always remember if it belonged to one of us,

It was understood to be ours.

Always remember, the love between us two,

The Us, not the me or the you.

Always remember how I loved you so

And the little things I did to let you know.

Always remember and keep peace in your heart,

For my love is a bond, never to be broken apart.

Aging Love

We may get older,

We may get wiser

And may God let us live.

Let us look back on yesterday,

And look forward to tomorrow.

In doing so…

May time bring forgiveness,

May wisdom bring love.

May the wisdom of tomorrow's love,

Take away the sorrow of today's.

Spirituals

Spirituality is in essence, the results of one's journey, it is a place or perception, resulting from one's experience, insight or discernment. We live our lives instinctively, repetitiously and carnally. We live and we learn, although learning does not come naturally, living on the other hand, does. Living can best be described as our carnality. Carnality pertains to or is characterized by the flesh or the body, its passions and desires.

The application of the knowledge we learn can best be described as our spirituality. Spirituality is a place or state of mind, beyond carnality or living. It relates to the place or degree to which we live or exist as a result of the attainment and application of the knowledge of life. A master of Israel, a man of power and position (carnality), sought out Jesus after seeing His spirituality. Jesus's response to him was:

John 3:6 &11 (KJV)
6 That which is born of the flesh is flesh; and that which is born of the Spirit is spirit.

11 Verily, verily, I say unto thee, We speak that we do know, and testify that we have seen; and ye receive not our witness.

The poems in this section are here because they were written from that point or place where knowledge is cultivated. I trust you will enjoy these poems. Whether you read them through carnal or spiritual eyes, I pray you are blessed by them.

Awakening the Dreamer

Do not talk to me of dreaming,
It's been a long time since I slept.
I am fully awake with vision,
Enough to know why Jesus wept.
I have walked the valley of hopelessness,
I have climbed mountains of despair.
I know what it means to be lost in darkness,
Bowing to and for everything, Except for prayer.
Don't talk to me of dreaming,
Of hope unfulfilled and destiny un-kept.
I, too have drunk from the cup of bitterness
And because I love you so I to wept.
If I could somehow shake you, shake you in the past,
I know you would awake.
See, you've been dreaming far too long,
Envision your dreams, make them reality.
For the night itself is against you,
You must see your visions today
Because when darkness comes,
Even dreamers lose their way.
We've all lost some things,
To include some sleep, along the way.
We have been frustrated by our dreams,
The ignorance of darkness, clouding our day.
Brothers, it's time out for dreaming,
Just ask Martin, today is the day.
Wake Up! Wake Up, you sleeping giant,
Wake Up! It's time you found your way.

Don't close your eyes,
Talking about a dream.
For if ever there was a man of vision,
It was Dr. Martin Luther King.
I say to you my brothers,
Wake-Up! The day the prophet's saw is near.
Jesus said, "I have overcome the world",
Martin said, "I have seen the promise land",
I say to you my dazed brothers,
"Wake-Up! The day of promise is at hand.
It's time we stood up in the valley,
And beheld the glorious light of day.
See, I have seen the mountaintop,
Only I was looking from the shadow of death.
I know the Way, the Truth and the Life,
The Drum Major made it all so bright.
I'm marching forward,
From darkness to light.
I have no time for dreaming,
My vision is in sight.
I too am a drum major,
In stride and in step,
Listening to the inner drum, within myself.
I know that I know
And I'm not dreaming anymore,
See, I have vision enough to share my light
With the world as a whole.

Oh Star

You stars up there,

You seem so many.

I bet in your lifetime,

You've seen plenty.

You stars way up there,

Why do you glow?

There must be a reason,

For putting on such a show.

You stars up there,

Ever so high,

Tell me,

Is it really heavenly in the sky?

You are a heavenly body,

That's what they say

And that even you,

Don't have your own way.

You stars, I've seen a few of you fall

And burn out, to suddenly,

Become nothing at all.

Others of you, hang around as though,

You have nowhere else, In the world to go.

You stars up there,

That glitter and shine,

I have seen the light of your life,

Have you seen the light of mine?

You stars up there,

Tell me, why do you stare?

I know as I'm looking up,

You're looking down here.

Oh star, Oh star, Oh star a glee,

Answer me quickly,

For day is coming indeed.

Center Piece

Take a star, place it high,

Take a star, place it in my eye.

Take a star and make it shine,

Take a star but don't take mine.

Take the sun and all its warm rays,

Take away darkness and all its mysterious ways.

Take the day and all its light,

Only leave me my star and all will work out right.

Return To Our Maker

God gave us all,
Two unavoidable paths to take.
A birth canal
And a journey back to our Maker.
Between the two, we are blessed,
With a lifetime to spend,
Being a blessing to others,
Before meeting our Maker again.
There is a time to live
And there is a time to die.
There is a time to laugh
And a time to cry.
Life and laughter,
Death and tears,
May God sweeten our sorrows
And comfort our fears.
God blessed us all,
With something precious of His.
We are eternally grateful
For the soul that has returned to Him.

Don't I Know You?

Don't I know you?
You smile and you grin.
Tell me, do I know you?
From where or when?
I know that we've met before.
Maybe in some time
And place we have both been.
Now that amazingly beautiful,
Smile of yours,
Such a beautiful canopy,
Truly to be adored.
I know that there's something deeper,
Could your smile be a canopy;
Hiding your doors?
We all have doors,
To enter in, out and through.
Some are just corridors,
A glance or distant view.
I've known doors
And the truth is I have a few,
Tell me, don't I know you?
Unknown

Within Love

In the few memories I have shared with you,
We find a disappointing answer and a loving Truth.
We discovered that which has been hidden for years,
Behind the deceit, temptation, lies, love and tears.
It is a rare discovery found only beyond one's fears,
It is a near, yet distant place, lovers have sought for years.
Few discover it, though they search for it a lifetime,
Our discovery was no more than a fortunate find.
We have nothing to show for it, for only we can behold,
The priceless moments that fill our mind, heart and soul.
Some may talk it down but the truth remain the truth.
That truth is, no matter what, I'll always love you".
Remember the strength of Joy, and the comfort of laughter,
I loved you yesterday and I've loved you every day after.
Amidst life's past deceits, temptation, lies or tears,
I now know that "within love" I can conqueror my fears.
Our days, there shall never be days as those we've known,
No matter where life leads us, we shall not be alone.
When your emotional skies are filled with clouds of doubt,
Remember with love, your strength is within, not without.

The Facts Are

You are Still…

Still the woman, I chose,

I Love So There is no question…

I love you for sure,

We have what it takes to endure.

The things I desire…

It's your happiness I desire most.

Above all things, I desire Righteousness,

Peace and Joy in the Holy Ghost.

For such is the Kingdom for me.

Love will be tried,

It must prove itself true.

In the midst of our trials,

Know that I still love you.

The Truth Is

No, you are not perfect,

Yes, you have a long way to go.

Yes, you are overly emotional,

Yes, You don't communicate well with me.

No, I'm not perfect either

Yes, I have even farther to go.

Yes, I am less emotional and

No, I have not mastered communication either.

But yes, I strive and work at perfection,

No! I am not there but I hope to be.

Yes, sometimes emotions get the best of me.

But yes, I still believe,

True love brings out the best in me.

Am I To Blame?

No one knows Me and Myself better than I,

For it's within me that the three lie.

I am often judged, along with Me and Myself,

When someone is to be blamed only I am left.

Me and Myself are but a part of I,

Neither can the other deny.

I have in this body Me and Myself combined,

If I make a mistake, why not blame Me,

For Myself knows the blame is surely mine.

But I ask, why do I get blamed all the time?

Student of Life

I was born a student of life,

A mind to be shaped and molded.

I was born into a world of intelligence,

I was born in ignorance, so I am told.

I have lived, I have learned, I now know,

That ignorance was belief in what I was told.

I am a student and life is my greatest teacher,

For knowledge is of the creator,

We are all creatures.

There is much to be said,

Even more to be known,

I now look in the dark glass,

Knowing the reflection I see will someday be my own.

Unknown

Sea Mates

As a sailor, one must sail life's many rough seas,

For my life is a sea, and I am a sailor indeed.

It is said, a true warrior will live to fight many wars,

The treasure I seek is not won in war but in love.

Life seems so brief as I look over my life span,

The distance I have come from boyhood to be a man.

Though I've come a long distance,

I must travel on having met you,

My heart refuses to travel alone.

Where is the sailor in me who would sail life's seas?

Where is the warrior who would battle life till eternity?

The sailor will not set to sea till you have come aboard?

The Warrior will not fight without the weapon of your love.

Join me on my ship as I travel life's many seas,

With you by my side, I'll battle life till death conquers me.

You are my treasure, for you are more precious than gold,

Set sail with me, my love,

Your heart, your mind your body and your Soul.

I Am

Yes, you know me, you are my past,

You are my present, to a degree.

Therefore, when all is said and done,

You know me.

Yes, you know me,

We've stepped out; over stepped; bound together,

Flowing like a shallow stream through the desert.

Yes, you know me,

You know my weaknesses as well as my strengths.

But as for who I AM,

You don't have a hint.

I have walked the earth among you,

Just as much a captive as yourself.

I've been a long time in the making,

But I AM, I have come unto myself.

I AM, the Greatest Creation of GOD.

Poetic Thoughts and Inspirations

Thoughts on the "Gift" Sections

Thoughts on the "Present Blessings" Section

Thoughts on the "Inspired By Love" Section

Thoughts on the "Love" Section

Thoughts on the "Wisdom" Sections

Made in the USA
Columbia, SC
29 August 2023

22178455R00067